Everyone Has A Song Anthem

A Black History Tribute to Bob Marley and Beyonce

Katie Canty

"Love God. Love People"

ISBN: 9798419009363

ACKNOWLEDGMENT

to all who inspire great things

with their time, talent,

technology, and/or treasure

Beyonce' and Bob Marley

Note: These two great performers

are acknowledged to say thanks

for the inspiration. Thanks.

DEDICATION

To ancestors

past, present, and future

Dedication
Black National Anthem Writer
James Weldon Johnson

Dedication
United States National Anthem Writer
Francis Scott Key

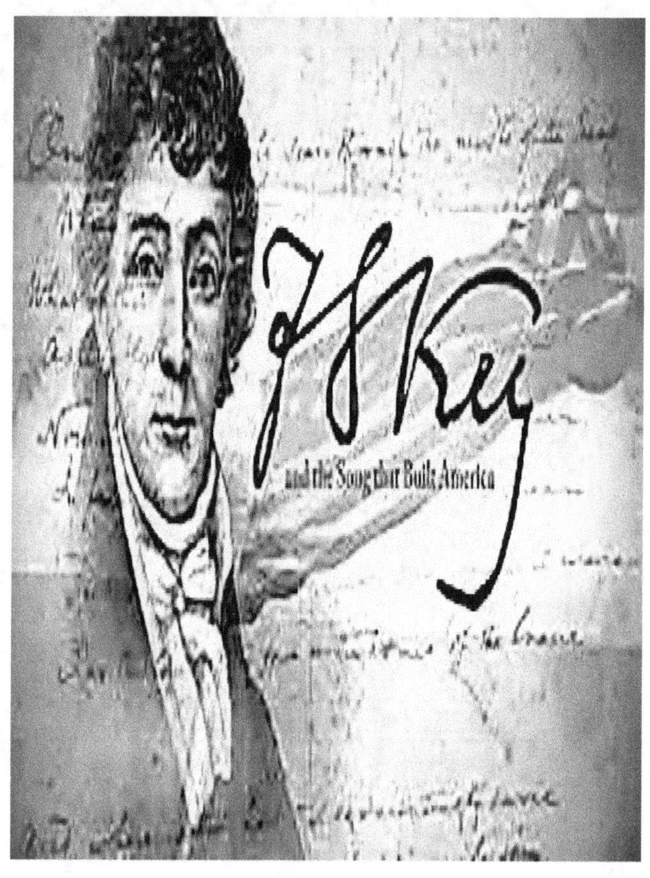

TABLE OF CONTENTS

Acknowledgments i

Females 6

Anthem Writers Society 7

Version 1 11

Version 2 15

About Anthems 17

About Black History 19

Will you just take a look at that? My Internet search does not come up with one single photo image--not one female national anthem song writer of color!

OK, it's time to change this.

I am starting a new thing—THE INTERNATIONAL ANTHEM WRITERS SOCIETY! Now you can find a multi-cultural female anthem writer.

Hello World, would a Society of National Anthem Writers be proud or sad about this female's newest, yet oldest, national anthem?

A mountain climber bro

named, Moses, might be

better than OK with these

two versions of the

humankind national anthem.

"What do you think, World?"

Island Style Version 1

HUMANKIND
NATIONAL ANTHEM

Verse #1

Let's get together and love

God Jehovah, and no other.

One God - got to love our

God Jehovah and not idol

another.

No man, no woman, no

kill each other.

Verse #2

True lies, no such thing say.

Momma, Poppa, honor to give, God say.

Hey man, hey woman, love the neighbor the way God say.

Verse #3

With the feet, heart, mind, spirit, Sabbath Day holiness, keep it.

No man, no woman, no stealing it.

Misuse God's name, no man, no woman--no can do.

Belongings of another, no want for me or for you.

VERSION 2
contemporary style
HUMANKIND
NATIONAL ANTHEM

Leave other gods alone.

Idols--just say no.

Misusing God's name is a
no, no.

Keep the Sabbath holy.

Honor Mom and Dad.

Murder—no can do.

Adultery—no way.

Steal a little, steal a lot?
Neither.

No making up lies about the neighbor.

No making googly eyes over another's stuff.

Love the neighbor as yourself.

With the heart, mind, and soul, show God some real love.

ABOUT NATIONAL ANTHEMS

The national anthem for the United States of America is "The Star-Spangled Banner" written as poem lyrics in 1814. The Black National Anthem, "Lift Every Voice and Sing" was a poem written by James Weldon Johnson in 1900.

Helen Reddy wrote "I Am Woman," and it became a feminist anthem in the 2000s. The

Humankind National Anthem Versions 1 and 2 is for the entire human race—people of every color! For thousands of years to present day, some nations and groups sing this anthem with their actions—not words.

What is a national anthem? Wikipedia shows this information.

...a patriotic musical composition that evokes and eulogizes the history, traditions, and struggles of its people, recognized either by a nation's government as the official national song, or by convention through use by the people

ABOUT BLACK HISTORY

Black history month acknowledges and honors African Americans whose inventions, accomplishments, or activism have a huge impact on making this world a much better place for all. Black history today is pretty much everyone's history.

Black history is the story of past, present, and future descendants of African American slaves. Can you imagine a place where your rights and freedom are based on the color of your skin?

In the United States of America in the 1950's and earlier, if you had black skin, you could not stay in hotels and could not eat inside restaurants. If you were a Black child you could only go to a special school like Williston, which was set aside just for Black children. You could not go to public places like the museum, library, park, or beach. If allowed to ride a bus, you sat in the back only. Black people worked very hard and paid taxes. But they did not get fair equal treatment or pay and could not even vote.

Descendants today who self-identify as Black may not look black in skin color at all. Children who are descendants of two black parents and raised in a Black church environment are very rapidly dwindling in USA communities.

ABOUT THE AUTHOR

Dr. Katie Canty, Ed.D.

Hello World,

Glad to meet you. I am amazed by what people can do globally and peacefully with the four T's—time, talent, treasure, technology. I teach grandparent populations that grew up without using computers how to use software and benefit from new technology.